CHILD OBSERVATION DATA FORM

Literacy

Name: ____

TEST DATE 1:

Examiner(s):

Comments:

TEST DATE 2:

Examiner(s):

Comments:

TEST DATE 3:

Examiner(s):

Comments:

Assessment, Evaluation, and Programming System for Infants and Children, Third Edition (AEPS®-3),
by Bricker, Dionne, Grisham, Johnson, Macy, Slentz, & Waddell. © 2022 Brookes Publishing Co. All rights reserved.

CHILD OBSERVATION DATA FORM

Math

Name: ______________________________

TEST DATE 1:

Examiner(s):

Comments:

TEST DATE 2:

Examiner(s):

Comments:

TEST DATE 3:

Examiner(s):

Comments:

Assessment, Evaluation, and Programming System for Infants and Children, Third Edition (AEPS®-3),
by Bricker, Dionne, Grisham, Johnson, Macy, Slentz, & Waddell. © 2022 Brookes Publishing Co. All rights reserved.

CHILD OBSERVATION DATA FORM

Gross Motor

Name: ______________________________

TEST DATE 1:

Examiner(s):

Comments:

TEST DATE 2:

Examiner(s):

Comments:

TEST DATE 3:

Examiner(s):

Comments:

Assessment, Evaluation, and Programming System for Infants and Children, Third Edition (AEPS®-3),
by Bricker, Dionne, Grisham, Johnson, Macy, Slentz, & Waddell. © 2022 Brookes Publishing Co. All rights reserved.

CHILD OBSERVATION DATA FORM

Fine Motor

Name: ____

TEST DATE 1:

Examiner(s):

Comments:

TEST DATE 2:

Examiner(s):

Comments:

TEST DATE 3:

Examiner(s):

Comments:

Assessment, Evaluation, and Programming System for Infants and Children, Third Edition (AEPS®-3),
by Bricker, Dionne, Grisham, Johnson, Macy, Slentz, & Waddell. © 2022 Brookes Publishing Co. All rights reserved.

Social-Emotional

Score Key			Note Key
Mastery performance 2	Emerging performance 1A = Assistance 1I = Incomplete 1AI = Assistance/Incomplete	No performance 0	C = Conduct M = Modification Q = Quality R = Report

Test date:			
Examiner(s):			

E. Meeting Social Expectations *(continued)*	Target	Score	Notes	Score	Notes	Score	Notes
4. Relates identifying information about self			C M Q R		C M Q R		C M Q R
4.1 States birthday			C M Q R		C M Q R		C M Q R
4.2 States age			C M Q R		C M Q R		C M Q R
4.3 Provides given name or nickname of self and others			C M Q R		C M Q R		C M Q R

Social-Emotional Results

To calculate Area Raw Score: Add the 2 and 1 scores in the Score column for the specific test date.
To calculate Area Percent Score: Divide the Area Raw Score by the Area Raw Score Possible, then multiply by 100.

Test date			
Area Raw Score			
Area Raw Score Possible	122	122	122
Area Percent Score			

Assessment, Evaluation, and Programming System for Infants and Children, Third Edition (AEPS®-3),
by Bricker, Dionne, Grisham, Johnson, Macy, Slentz, & Waddell. © 2022 Brookes Publishing Co. All rights reserved.

Summary of AEPS-3 Results

Name: ____

For each area, plot the percent correct and indicate each test date to determine if the child's performance is improving over time.

Fine Motor

Total % correct			
100			
80			
60			
40			
20			
Test date:			

Gross Motor

Total % correct			
100			
80			
60			
40			
20			
Test date:			

Adaptive

Total % correct			
100			
80			
60			
40			
20			
Test date:			

Social-Emotional

Total % correct			
100			
80			
60			
40			
20			
Test date:			

Social-Communication

Total % correct			
100			
80			
60			
40			
20			
Test date:			

Cognitive

Total % correct			
100			
80			
60			
40			
20			
Test date:			

Literacy

Total % correct			
100			
80			
60			
40			
20			
Test date:			

Math

Total % correct			
100			
80			
60			
40			
20			
Test date:			

Assessment, Evaluation, and Programming System for Infants and Children, Third Edition (AEPS®-3),
by Bricker, Dionne, Grisham, Johnson, Macy, Slentz, & Waddell. © 2022 Brookes Publishing Co. All rights reserved.

Child Observation Data Form (CODF)

Date(s) completed: ____________________

Child's name: ____________________

Child's date of birth: ____________________

Child's ID: ____________________

Family's name and address: ____________________

____

Person completing form: ____________________

Program: ____________________

DIRECTIONS:

REVIEW the test administration information beginning on page 9 of AEPS-3 Volume 2, Chapter 2. Review item criteria, illustrations, examples, and notes beginning on page 34 of AEPS-3 Volume 2, Chapter 3. Make sure you understand the methods for collecting child performance data and scoring procedures before using this form.

RECORD the test administration date and examiner initials at the top of each AEPS-3 area (Fine Motor, Gross Motor, Adaptive, Social-Emotional, Social-Communication, Cognitive, Literacy, and Math).

OBSERVE the child and score AEPS-3 Test items by comparing the child's performance on each item with its stated criterion. Scoring items without using the stated criteria will invalidate the test results.

ENTER all item scores in the Score column and notes in the Notes column. Follow these rules for scoring the AEPS-3 Test to obtain valid assessment results:

- Score all goals.
- Assign only scores of 2, 1, or 0.
- If you assess and score a goal 2, score all objectives under that goal 2 without assessing each objective.
- If you assess and score a goal 1 or 0, assess and score all associated objectives.
- If you assess and score a goal or objective 1, you must assign an A, I, or both:
    - Use A if the child requires some form of assistance to perform the item.
    - Use I if the child's performance of the skill is incomplete (partial performance or inconsistent use of the skill).
- Use Notes to assist in qualifying children's scores (optional but highly recommended). Notes are as follows: C = Conduct; M = Modification; Q = Quality; R = Report.
- Target column refers to identified IEP or IFSP goal. Check this box for every selected goal.

RECORD the child's results at the end of each area (Area Raw Score and Area Percent Score). Also record comments as needed.

Assessment, Evaluation, and Programming System for Infants and Children, Third Edition (AEPS®-3),
by Bricker, Dionne, Grisham, Johnson, Macy, Slentz, & Waddell. © 2022 Brookes Publishing Co. All rights reserved.

CHILD OBSERVATION DATA FORM

Fine Motor

Name: ______________________________

Score Key			Note Key
Mastery performance 2	Emerging performance 1A = Assistance 1I = Incomplete 1AI = Assistance/Incomplete	No performance 0	C = Conduct M = Modification Q = Quality R = Report

Test date:			
Examiner(s):			

A. Reach, Grasp, and Release	Target	Score	Notes	Score	Notes	Score	Notes
1. Makes directed batting or swiping movements with each hand			C M Q R		C M Q R		C M Q R
1.1 Brings hands together near midline			C M Q R		C M Q R		C M Q R
1.2 Makes directed movements with arms			C M Q R		C M Q R		C M Q R
2. Grasps pea-size object			C M Q R		C M Q R		C M Q R
2.1 Grasps hand-size object			C M Q R		C M Q R		C M Q R
2.2 Grasps small cylindrical object			C M Q R		C M Q R		C M Q R
2.3 Grasps pea-size object using fingers in raking or scratching movement			C M Q R		C M Q R		C M Q R
2.4 Grasps hand-size object using whole hand			C M Q R		C M Q R		C M Q R
3. Stacks objects			C M Q R		C M Q R		C M Q R
3.1 Releases object into targeted space			C M Q R		C M Q R		C M Q R
3.2 Releases object into nondefined space			C M Q R		C M Q R		C M Q R
B. Functional Skill Use							
1. Activates object with finger			C M Q R		C M Q R		C M Q R
1.1 Uses finger to point or touch			C M Q R		C M Q R		C M Q R
1.2 Uses hand to activate object			C M Q R		C M Q R		C M Q R
1.3 Uses fingers to explore object			C M Q R		C M Q R		C M Q R
2. Rotates wrist to manipulate object			C M Q R		C M Q R		C M Q R
2.1 Turns object using either hand			C M Q R		C M Q R		C M Q R
3. Manipulates object with two hands, each performing different action			C M Q R		C M Q R		C M Q R
3.1 Assembles toy			C M Q R		C M Q R		C M Q R
3.2 Aligns objects			C M Q R		C M Q R		C M Q R

Assessment, Evaluation, and Programming System for Infants and Children, Third Edition (AEPS®-3),
by Bricker, Dionne, Grisham, Johnson, Macy, Slentz, & Waddell. © 2022 Brookes Publishing Co. All rights reserved.

Fine Motor

aeps 3

Score Key			Note Key
Mastery performance 2	Emerging performance 1A = Assistance 1I = Incomplete 1AI = Assistance/Incomplete	No performance 0	C = Conduct M = Modification Q = Quality R = Report

	Test date:			
	Examiner(s):			

B. Functional Skill Use *(continued)*	Target	Score	Notes	Score	Notes	Score	Notes
3.3 Fits variety of shapes into corresponding spaces			C M Q R		C M Q R		C M Q R
3.4 Holds object with one hand and manipulates object or produces action with other hand			C M Q R		C M Q R		C M Q R
3.5 Transfers object from hand to hand			C M Q R		C M Q R		C M Q R
C. Mechanics of Writing							
1. Holds writing tool using three-finger grasp to write or draw			C M Q R		C M Q R		C M Q R
1.1 Writes or draws using mixed strokes			C M Q R		C M Q R		C M Q R
1.2 Writes or draws using curved lines			C M Q R		C M Q R		C M Q R
1.3 Writes or draws using straight lines			C M Q R		C M Q R		C M Q R
1.4 Scribbles			C M Q R		C M Q R		C M Q R
D. Use of Electronic Devices							
1. Uses finger to interact with electronic device			C M Q R		C M Q R		C M Q R
1.1 Uses finger to interact with simple electronic game			C M Q R		C M Q R		C M Q R
1.2 Uses finger to interact with touch screen			C M Q R		C M Q R		C M Q R

Fine Motor Results

To calculate Area Raw Score: Add the 2 and 1 scores in the Score column for the specific test date.
To calculate Area Percent Score: Divide the Area Raw Score by the Area Raw Score Possible, then multiply by 100.

Test date			
Area Raw Score			
Area Raw Score Possible	62	62	62
Area Percent Score			

Assessment, Evaluation, and Programming System for Infants and Children, Third Edition (AEPS®-3),
by Bricker, Dionne, Grisham, Johnson, Macy, Slentz, & Waddell. © 2022 Brookes Publishing Co. All rights reserved.

Fine Motor

Name: ____

TEST DATE 1:

Examiner(s):

Comments:

TEST DATE 2:

Examiner(s):

Comments:

TEST DATE 3:

Examiner(s):

Comments:

Assessment, Evaluation, and Programming System for Infants and Children, Third Edition (AEPS®-3),
by Bricker, Dionne, Grisham, Johnson, Macy, Slentz, & Waddell. © 2022 Brookes Publishing Co. All rights reserved.

CHILD OBSERVATION DATA FORM

Gross Motor

aeps-3

Name: ______________________________

Score Key			Note Key
Mastery performance 2	Emerging performance 1A = Assistance 1I = Incomplete 1AI = Assistance/Incomplete	No performance 0	C = Conduct M = Modification Q = Quality R = Report

Test date:			
Examiner(s):			

A. Body Control and Weight Transfer	Target	Score	Notes	Score	Notes	Score	Notes
1. Turns head, moves arms, and kicks legs independently of each other			C M Q R		C M Q R		C M Q R
1.1 Kicks legs			C M Q R		C M Q R		C M Q R
1.2 Waves arms			C M Q R		C M Q R		C M Q R
1.3 Turns head side to side			C M Q R		C M Q R		C M Q R
2. Puts weight on one hand or arm while reaching with opposite hand			C M Q R		C M Q R		C M Q R
2.1 Remains propped on extended arms with head lifted			C M Q R		C M Q R		C M Q R
2.2 Remains propped on nonextended forearms with head lifted			C M Q R		C M Q R		C M Q R
3. Rolls from back to stomach			C M Q R		C M Q R		C M Q R
3.1 Rolls from stomach to back			C M Q R		C M Q R		C M Q R
3.2 Rolls from back or stomach to side			C M Q R		C M Q R		C M Q R
4. Assumes balanced sitting position			C M Q R		C M Q R		C M Q R
4.1 Assumes hands-and-knees position from sitting			C M Q R		C M Q R		C M Q R
4.2 Regains balanced, upright sitting position after reaching across body			C M Q R		C M Q R		C M Q R
4.3 Regains balanced, upright sitting position after leaning left, right, and forward			C M Q R		C M Q R		C M Q R
4.4 Sits balanced without support			C M Q R		C M Q R		C M Q R
4.5 Sits balanced using hands for support			C M Q R		C M Q R		C M Q R
4.6 Holds head in midline when sitting supported			C M Q R		C M Q R		C M Q R
5. Gets out of chair			C M Q R		C M Q R		C M Q R
5.1 Sits down in chair			C M Q R		C M Q R		C M Q R
5.2 Maintains sitting position in chair			C M Q R		C M Q R		C M Q R

Assessment, Evaluation, and Programming System for Infants and Children, Third Edition (AEPS®-3),
by Bricker, Dionne, Grisham, Johnson, Macy, Slentz, & Waddell. © 2022 Brookes Publishing Co. All rights reserved.

Gross Motor

Score Key			Note Key
Mastery performance 2	Emerging performance 1A = Assistance 1I = Incomplete 1AI = Assistance/Incomplete	No performance 0	C = Conduct M = Modification Q = Quality R = Report

Test date:			
Examiner(s):			

B. Movement and Coordination	Target	Score	Notes	Score	Notes	Score	Notes
1. Creeps forward using alternating arm and leg movements			C M Q R		C M Q R		C M Q R
1.1 Rocks while in creeping position			C M Q R		C M Q R		C M Q R
1.2 Assumes creeping position			C M Q R		C M Q R		C M Q R
1.3 Crawls forward on stomach			C M Q R		C M Q R		C M Q R
1.4 Pivots on stomach			C M Q R		C M Q R		C M Q R
2. Stoops and regains balanced standing position			C M Q R		C M Q R		C M Q R
2.1 Rises from sitting to standing position			C M Q R		C M Q R		C M Q R
2.2 Stands unsupported			C M Q R		C M Q R		C M Q R
2.3 Pulls to standing position			C M Q R		C M Q R		C M Q R
2.4 Pulls to kneeling position			C M Q R		C M Q R		C M Q R
3. Walks avoiding people, furniture, or objects			C M Q R		C M Q R		C M Q R
3.1 Walks without support			C M Q R		C M Q R		C M Q R
3.2 Walks with one-hand support			C M Q R		C M Q R		C M Q R
3.3 Walks with two-hand support			C M Q R		C M Q R		C M Q R
3.4 Cruises			C M Q R		C M Q R		C M Q R
4. Alternates feet going up and down stairs			C M Q R		C M Q R		C M Q R
4.1 Walks up and down stairs using support			C M Q R		C M Q R		C M Q R
4.2 Moves up and down stairs			C M Q R		C M Q R		C M Q R
4.3 Gets up and down from low structure			C M Q R		C M Q R		C M Q R

Assessment, Evaluation, and Programming System for Infants and Children, Third Edition (AEPS®-3),
by Bricker, Dionne, Grisham, Johnson, Macy, Slentz, & Waddell. © 2022 Brookes Publishing Co. All rights reserved.

CHILD OBSERVATION DATA FORM

Gross Motor

aeps3

Score Key			Note Key
Mastery performance 2	Emerging performance 1A = Assistance 1I = Incomplete 1AI = Assistance/Incomplete	No performance 0	C = Conduct M = Modification Q = Quality R = Report

Test date:			
Examiner(s):			

B. Movement and Coordination *(continued)*	Target	Score	Notes	Score	Notes	Score	Notes
5. Runs while avoiding people, furniture, or other objects			C M Q R		C M Q R		C M Q R
5.1 Runs			C M Q R		C M Q R		C M Q R
5.2 Walks fast			C M Q R		C M Q R		C M Q R
6. Jumps forward			C M Q R		C M Q R		C M Q R
6.1 Jumps up and down in place			C M Q R		C M Q R		C M Q R
6.2 Jumps down from low structure			C M Q R		C M Q R		C M Q R
6.3 Jumps down with support			C M Q R		C M Q R		C M Q R
7. Skips			C M Q R		C M Q R		C M Q R
7.1 Gallops			C M Q R		C M Q R		C M Q R
7.2 Hops forward on one foot			C M Q R		C M Q R		C M Q R
C. Active Play							
1. Swings bat, club, or stick to strike stationary object			C M Q R		C M Q R		C M Q R
1.1 Bounces ball with one hand			C M Q R		C M Q R		C M Q R
1.2 Bounces ball with two hands			C M Q R		C M Q R		C M Q R
1.3 Catches ball			C M Q R		C M Q R		C M Q R
1.4 Kicks ball			C M Q R		C M Q R		C M Q R
1.5 Throws ball overhand at target with one hand			C M Q R		C M Q R		C M Q R
1.6 Throws or rolls ball at target with two hands			C M Q R		C M Q R		C M Q R

Assessment, Evaluation, and Programming System for Infants and Children, Third Edition (AEPS®-3),
by Bricker, Dionne, Grisham, Johnson, Macy, Slentz, & Waddell. © 2022 Brookes Publishing Co. All rights reserved.

Gross Motor

Score Key			Note Key
Mastery performance 2	Emerging performance 1A = Assistance 1I = Incomplete 1AI = Assistance/Incomplete	No performance 0	C = Conduct M = Modification Q = Quality R = Report

Test date:			
Examiner(s):			

C. Active Play *(continued)*	Target	Score	Notes	Score	Notes	Score	Notes
2. Uses hands to hang on play equipment with bars			C M Q R		C M Q R		C M Q R
2.1 Moves swing back and forth			C M Q R		C M Q R		C M Q R
2.2 Climbs play equipment			C M Q R		C M Q R		C M Q R
2.3 Goes down small slide			C M Q R		C M Q R		C M Q R
3. Rides and steers bicycle			C M Q R		C M Q R		C M Q R
3.1 Pedals and steers bicycle with training wheels			C M Q R		C M Q R		C M Q R
3.2 Pedals and steers tricycle			C M Q R		C M Q R		C M Q R
3.3 Pushes riding toy with feet while steering			C M Q R		C M Q R		C M Q R
3.4 Sits on riding toy or in wagon while in motion			C M Q R		C M Q R		C M Q R

Gross Motor Results

To calculate Area Raw Score: Add the 2 and 1 scores in the Score column for the specific test date.
To calculate Area Percent Score: Divide the Area Raw Score by the Area Raw Score Possible, then multiply by 100.

Test date			
Area Raw Score			
Area Raw Score Possible	130	130	130
Area Percent Score			

Assessment, Evaluation, and Programming System for Infants and Children, Third Edition (AEPS®-3),
by Bricker, Dionne, Grisham, Johnson, Macy, Slentz, & Waddell. © 2022 Brookes Publishing Co. All rights reserved.

Gross Motor

Name: ______________________________

TEST DATE 1:

Examiner(s):

Comments:

TEST DATE 2:

Examiner(s):

Comments:

TEST DATE 3:

Examiner(s):

Comments:

Assessment, Evaluation, and Programming System for Infants and Children, Third Edition (AEPS®-3),
by Bricker, Dionne, Grisham, Johnson, Macy, Slentz, & Waddell. © 2022 Brookes Publishing Co. All rights reserved.

CHILD OBSERVATION DATA FORM

Adaptive

aeps-3

Name: ____________________

Score Key			Note Key
Mastery performance 2	Emerging performance 1A = Assistance 1I = Incomplete 1AI = Assistance/Incomplete	No performance 0	C = Conduct M = Modification Q = Quality R = Report

Test date:			
Examiner(s):			

A. Eating and Drinking	Target	Score	Notes	Score	Notes	Score	Notes
1. Uses lips to take semisolid foods off eating utensil			C M Q R		C M Q R		C M Q R
1.1 Swallows semisolid foods			C M Q R		C M Q R		C M Q R
1.2 Swallows liquids			C M Q R		C M Q R		C M Q R
2. Eats foods from variety of food groups with variety of textures			C M Q R		C M Q R		C M Q R
2.1 Eats hard and chewy foods			C M Q R		C M Q R		C M Q R
2.2 Eats crisp foods			C M Q R		C M Q R		C M Q R
2.3 Eats soft and dissolvable foods			C M Q R		C M Q R		C M Q R
3. Eats with eating utensils			C M Q R		C M Q R		C M Q R
3.1 Brings food to mouth with eating utensil			C M Q R		C M Q R		C M Q R
3.2 Eats with fingers			C M Q R		C M Q R		C M Q R
3.3 Accepts food presented on eating utensils			C M Q R		C M Q R		C M Q R
4. Drinks from open-mouth container			C M Q R		C M Q R		C M Q R
4.1 Drinks from cup with spouted lid			C M Q R		C M Q R		C M Q R
4.2 Drinks from container held by adult			C M Q R		C M Q R		C M Q R
5. Uses culturally appropriate social dining skills			C M Q R		C M Q R		C M Q R
5.1 Puts appropriate amount of food in mouth, chews, and swallows before taking another bite			C M Q R		C M Q R		C M Q R
5.2 Takes in appropriate amount of liquid and returns cup to surface			C M Q R		C M Q R		C M Q R
6. Prepares food for eating			C M Q R		C M Q R		C M Q R
6.1 Pours liquid into variety of containers			C M Q R		C M Q R		C M Q R
6.2 Serves food with utensil			C M Q R		C M Q R		C M Q R

Assessment, Evaluation, and Programming System for Infants and Children, Third Edition (AEPS®-3),
by Bricker, Dionne, Grisham, Johnson, Macy, Slentz, & Waddell. © 2022 Brookes Publishing Co. All rights reserved.

CHILD OBSERVATION DATA FORM

Adaptive

aeps-3

Score Key			Note Key
Mastery performance 2	Emerging performance 1A = Assistance 1I = Incomplete 1AI = Assistance/Incomplete	No performance 0	C = Conduct M = Modification Q = Quality R = Report

Test date:			
Examiner(s):			

B. Personal Care Routines	Target	Score	Notes	Score	Notes	Score	Notes
1. Carries out all toileting functions			C M Q R		C M Q R		C M Q R
1.1 Indicates need to use toilet			C M Q R		C M Q R		C M Q R
1.2 Has bowel and bladder control			C M Q R		C M Q R		C M Q R
1.3 Indicates awareness of soiled and wet pants or diapers			C M Q R		C M Q R		C M Q R
2. Bathes and dries self			C M Q R		C M Q R		C M Q R
2.1 Washes and dries face			C M Q R		C M Q R		C M Q R
2.2 Washes and dries hands			C M Q R		C M Q R		C M Q R
3. Completes all steps for personal hygiene, including brushing teeth, combing hair, and wiping nose			C M Q R		C M Q R		C M Q R
3.1 Completes some steps to brush teeth, comb hair, and wipe nose			C M Q R		C M Q R		C M Q R
C. Dressing and Undressing							
1. Undresses self by removing all clothing			C M Q R		C M Q R		C M Q R
1.1 Unfastens clothing			C M Q R		C M Q R		C M Q R
1.2 Takes off pullover clothing over head			C M Q R		C M Q R		C M Q R
1.3 Takes off front-opening coat, jacket, or shirt			C M Q R		C M Q R		C M Q R
1.4 Takes off pants			C M Q R		C M Q R		C M Q R
1.5 Takes off shoes			C M Q R		C M Q R		C M Q R
1.6 Takes off socks			C M Q R		C M Q R		C M Q R
1.7 Takes off hat			C M Q R		C M Q R		C M Q R
2. Selects appropriate clothing and dresses self			C M Q R		C M Q R		C M Q R
2.1 Fastens clothing			C M Q R		C M Q R		C M Q R
2.2 Puts on front-opening clothing			C M Q R		C M Q R		C M Q R

Assessment, Evaluation, and Programming System for Infants and Children, Third Edition (AEPS®-3),
by Bricker, Dionne, Grisham, Johnson, Macy, Slentz, & Waddell. © 2022 Brookes Publishing Co. All rights reserved.

Adaptive

Score Key			Note Key
Mastery performance 2	Emerging performance 1A = Assistance 1I = Incomplete 1AI = Assistance/Incomplete	No performance 0	C = Conduct M = Modification Q = Quality R = Report

	Test date:					
	Examiner(s):					
C. Dressing and Undressing *(continued)*	**Target**	**Score**	**Notes**	**Score**	**Notes**	**Score**	**Notes**
2.3 Puts on pullover clothing			C M Q R		C M Q R		C M Q R
2.4 Puts on pull-up clothing			C M Q R		C M Q R		C M Q R
2.5 Puts on socks			C M Q R		C M Q R		C M Q R
2.6 Puts on shoes			C M Q R		C M Q R		C M Q R
D. Personal Safety							
1. Takes independent action to alleviate distress, discomfort, and pain			C M Q R		C M Q R		C M Q R
1.1 Communicates internal distress, discomfort, or pain to adult			C M Q R		C M Q R		C M Q R
2. Complies with common home and community safety rules			C M Q R		C M Q R		C M Q R
2.1 Complies with graphic or written warning signs and symbols			C M Q R		C M Q R		C M Q R
3. Takes independent action when faced with dangerous conditions or substances			C M Q R		C M Q R		C M Q R
3.1 Responds appropriately to warnings of dangerous conditions or substances			C M Q R		C M Q R		C M Q R
4. Recognizes and reports information regarding safety			C M Q R		C M Q R		C M Q R
4.1 States or produces personal information to promote/maintain personal safety			C M Q R		C M Q R		C M Q R
4.2 Reports inappropriate events, actions, or language by others			C M Q R		C M Q R		C M Q R

Adaptive Results

To calculate Area Raw Score: Add the 2 and 1 scores in the Score column for the specific test date.
To calculate Area Percent Score: Divide the Area Raw Score by the Area Raw Score Possible, then multiply by 100.

Test date			
Area Raw Score			
Area Raw Score Possible	106	106	106
Area Percent Score			

Assessment, Evaluation, and Programming System for Infants and Children, Third Edition (AEPS®-3),
by Bricker, Dionne, Grisham, Johnson, Macy, Slentz, & Waddell. © 2022 Brookes Publishing Co. All rights reserved.

CHILD OBSERVATION DATA FORM

Adaptive

Name: ______________________________

TEST DATE 1:

Examiner(s):

Comments:

TEST DATE 2:

Examiner(s):

Comments:

TEST DATE 3:

Examiner(s):

Comments:

Assessment, Evaluation, and Programming System for Infants and Children, Third Edition (AEPS®-3),
by Bricker, Dionne, Grisham, Johnson, Macy, Slentz, & Waddell. © 2022 Brookes Publishing Co. All rights reserved.

CHILD OBSERVATION DATA FORM

Social-Emotional

aeps®3

Name: ____________________

Score Key			Note Key
Mastery performance 2	Emerging performance 1A = Assistance 1I = Incomplete 1AI = Assistance/Incomplete	No performance 0	C = Conduct M = Modification Q = Quality R = Report

Test date:			
Examiner(s):			

A. Interactions with Adults	Target	Score	Notes	Score	Notes	Score	Notes
1. Initiates positive social behavior toward familiar adult			C M Q R		C M Q R		C M Q R
1.1 Responds appropriately to familiar adult's affective tone			C M Q R		C M Q R		C M Q R
1.2 Responds to familiar adult's positive social behavior			C M Q R		C M Q R		C M Q R
2. Maintains social interaction with familiar adult			C M Q R		C M Q R		C M Q R
2.1 Initiates simple social interaction with familiar adult			C M Q R		C M Q R		C M Q R
2.2 Repeats part of interactive game or action in order to continue game or action			C M Q R		C M Q R		C M Q R
2.3 Responds to familiar game or action			C M Q R		C M Q R		C M Q R
3. Participates in familiar social routines with caregivers			C M Q R		C M Q R		C M Q R
3.1 Initiates next step of familiar social routine			C M Q R		C M Q R		C M Q R
3.2 Follows familiar social routines with familiar adults			C M Q R		C M Q R		C M Q R
B. Social-Emotional Expression and Regulation							
1. Responds appropriately to others' emotions			C M Q R		C M Q R		C M Q R
1.1 Identifies/labels emotions in others			C M Q R		C M Q R		C M Q R
1.2 Identifies/labels own emotions			C M Q R		C M Q R		C M Q R
2. Uses appropriate strategies to manage emotional states			C M Q R		C M Q R		C M Q R
2.1 Responds appropriately to soothing by peer			C M Q R		C M Q R		C M Q R
2.2 Seeks comfort, closeness, or physical contact from familiar adult			C M Q R		C M Q R		C M Q R
2.3 Responds appropriately to soothing by adult			C M Q R		C M Q R		C M Q R
3. Makes positive statements about self or accomplishments			C M Q R		C M Q R		C M Q R
3.1 Explains or shows others how to do tasks mastered			C M Q R		C M Q R		C M Q R
3.2 Shares accomplishment with familiar caregiver			C M Q R		C M Q R		C M Q R

Assessment, Evaluation, and Programming System for Infants and Children, Third Edition (AEPS®-3),
by Bricker, Dionne, Grisham, Johnson, Macy, Slentz, & Waddell. © 2022 Brookes Publishing Co. All rights reserved.

Social-Emotional

Score Key			Note Key
Mastery performance 2	Emerging performance 1A = Assistance 1I = Incomplete 1AI = Assistance/Incomplete	No performance 0	C = Conduct M = Modification Q = Quality R = Report

Test date:			
Examiner(s):			

C. Interactions with Peers	Target	Score	Notes	Score	Notes	Score	Notes
1. Maintains interaction with peer			C M Q R		C M Q R		C M Q R
1.1 Initiates social behavior toward peer			C M Q R		C M Q R		C M Q R
1.2 Responds appropriately to peer social behavior			C M Q R		C M Q R		C M Q R
1.3 Plays near one or two peers			C M Q R		C M Q R		C M Q R
2. Plans and acts out recognizable event, theme, or storyline in imaginary play			C M Q R		C M Q R		C M Q R
2.1 Enacts roles or identities in imaginary play			C M Q R		C M Q R		C M Q R
2.2 Uses imaginary props in play			C M Q R		C M Q R		C M Q R
3. Maintains cooperative activity			C M Q R		C M Q R		C M Q R
3.1 Initiates cooperative activity			C M Q R		C M Q R		C M Q R
3.2 Joins others in cooperative activity			C M Q R		C M Q R		C M Q R
3.3 Shares or exchanges objects			C M Q R		C M Q R		C M Q R
4. Maintains engagement in games with rules			C M Q R		C M Q R		C M Q R
4.1 Knows and follows game rules			C M Q R		C M Q R		C M Q R
4.2 Participates in game			C M Q R		C M Q R		C M Q R
D. Independent and Group Participation							
1. Interacts appropriately with others during small-group activities			C M Q R		C M Q R		C M Q R
1.1 Interacts appropriately with materials during small-group activities			C M Q R		C M Q R		C M Q R
1.2 Responds appropriately to directions during small-group activities			C M Q R		C M Q R		C M Q R
1.3 Remains with group during small-group activities			C M Q R		C M Q R		C M Q R

Assessment, Evaluation, and Programming System for Infants and Children, Third Edition (AEPS®-3),
by Bricker, Dionne, Grisham, Johnson, Macy, Slentz, & Waddell. © 2022 Brookes Publishing Co. All rights reserved.

Social-Emotional

Score Key			Note Key
Mastery performance 2	Emerging performance 1A = Assistance 1I = Incomplete 1AI = Assistance/Incomplete	No performance 0	C = Conduct M = Modification Q = Quality R = Report

Test date:			
Examiner(s):			

D. Independent and Group Participation *(continued)*	Target	Score	Notes	Score	Notes	Score	Notes
2. Interacts appropriately with others during large-group activities			C M Q R		C M Q R		C M Q R
2.1 Interacts appropriately with materials during large-group activities			C M Q R		C M Q R		C M Q R
2.2 Responds appropriately to directions during large-group activities			C M Q R		C M Q R		C M Q R
2.3 Remains with group during large-group activities			C M Q R		C M Q R		C M Q R
3. Initiates and completes independent activities			C M Q R		C M Q R		C M Q R
3.1 Responds to request to finish activity			C M Q R		C M Q R		C M Q R
3.2 Responds to request to begin activity			C M Q R		C M Q R		C M Q R
3.3 Entertains self by playing with toys			C M Q R		C M Q R		C M Q R
4. Resolves conflicts using negotiation			C M Q R		C M Q R		C M Q R
4.1 Uses strategies to resolve conflicts			C M Q R		C M Q R		C M Q R
4.2 Claims and defends possessions			C M Q R		C M Q R		C M Q R
E. Meeting Social Expectations							
1. Meets observable physical needs in socially appropriate ways			C M Q R		C M Q R		C M Q R
1.1 Meets internal physical needs of hunger and thirst			C M Q R		C M Q R		C M Q R
2. Meets accepted social norms in community settings			C M Q R		C M Q R		C M Q R
2.1 Meets behavioral expectations in familiar environments			C M Q R		C M Q R		C M Q R
2.2 Adjusts behavior based on feedback from others or environment			C M Q R		C M Q R		C M Q R
3. Follows context-specific rules			C M Q R		C M Q R		C M Q R
3.1 Seeks adult permission when appropriate			C M Q R		C M Q R		C M Q R
3.2 Follows established social rules in familiar environments			C M Q R		C M Q R		C M Q R

Assessment, Evaluation, and Programming System for Infants and Children, Third Edition (AEPS®-3),
by Bricker, Dionne, Grisham, Johnson, Macy, Slentz, & Waddell. © 2022 Brookes Publishing Co. All rights reserved.

Social-Emotional

Score Key			Note Key
Mastery performance 2	Emerging performance 1A = Assistance 1I = Incomplete 1AI = Assistance/Incomplete	No performance 0	C = Conduct M = Modification Q = Quality R = Report

Test date:			
Examiner(s):			

E. Meeting Social Expectations *(continued)*	Target	Score	Notes	Score	Notes	Score	Notes
4. Relates identifying information about self			C M Q R		C M Q R		C M Q R
4.1 States birthday			C M Q R		C M Q R		C M Q R
4.2 States age			C M Q R		C M Q R		C M Q R
4.3 Provides given name or nickname of self and others			C M Q R		C M Q R		C M Q R

Social-Emotional Results

To calculate Area Raw Score: Add the 2 and 1 scores in the Score column for the specific test date.

To calculate Area Percent Score: Divide the Area Raw Score by the Area Raw Score Possible, then multiply by 100.

Test date			
Area Raw Score			
Area Raw Score Possible	122	122	122
Area Percent Score			

by Bricker, Dionne, Grisham, Johnson, Macy, Slentz, & Waddell. © 2022 Brookes Publishing Co. All rights reserved.

Social-Emotional

Name: ______________________________

TEST DATE 1:

Examiner(s):

Comments:

TEST DATE 2:

Examiner(s):

Comments:

TEST DATE 3:

Examiner(s):

Comments:

Assessment, Evaluation, and Programming System for Infants and Children, Third Edition (AEPS®-3),
by Bricker, Dionne, Grisham, Johnson, Macy, Slentz, & Waddell. © 2022 Brookes Publishing Co. All rights reserved.

CHILD OBSERVATION DATA FORM

Social-Communication

Name: ______________________________

Score Key			Note Key
Mastery performance 2	Emerging performance 1A = Assistance 1I = Incomplete 1AI = Assistance/Incomplete	No performance 0	C = Conduct M = Modification Q = Quality R = Report

Test date:			
Examiner(s):			

A. Early Social Communication	Target	Score	Notes	Score	Notes	Score	Notes
1. Turns and looks toward person speaking			C M Q R		C M Q R		C M Q R
1.1 Quiets to familiar voice			C M Q R		C M Q R		C M Q R
2. Produces speech sounds			C M Q R		C M Q R		C M Q R
2.1 Coos and gurgles			C M Q R		C M Q R		C M Q R
3. Engages in vocal exchanges			C M Q R		C M Q R		C M Q R
3.1 Vocalizes to another person expressing positive affective state			C M Q R		C M Q R		C M Q R
3.2 Vocalizes to another person expressing negative affective state			C M Q R		C M Q R		C M Q R
4. Uses intentional gestures, vocalizations, and objects to communicate			C M Q R		C M Q R		C M Q R
4.1 Makes requests of others			C M Q R		C M Q R		C M Q R
4.2 Makes choices to express preferences			C M Q R		C M Q R		C M Q R
4.3 Expresses desire to continue activity			C M Q R		C M Q R		C M Q R
4.4 Expresses negation or protests			C M Q R		C M Q R		C M Q R
B. Communicative Understanding							
1. Follows gaze to establish joint attention			C M Q R		C M Q R		C M Q R
1.1 Follows pointing gestures with eyes			C M Q R		C M Q R		C M Q R
1.2 Looks toward object			C M Q R		C M Q R		C M Q R
2. Locates common objects, people, or events			C M Q R		C M Q R		C M Q R
2.1 Recognizes own and familiar names			C M Q R		C M Q R		C M Q R
2.2 Responds to single-word directive			C M Q R		C M Q R		C M Q R

Assessment, Evaluation, and Programming System for Infants and Children, Third Edition (AEPS®-3),
by Bricker, Dionne, Grisham, Johnson, Macy, Slentz, & Waddell. © 2022 Brookes Publishing Co. All rights reserved.

Social-Communication

aeps3

Score Key			Note Key
Mastery performance 2	Emerging performance 1A = Assistance 1I = Incomplete 1AI = Assistance/Incomplete	No performance 0	C = Conduct M = Modification Q = Quality R = Report

Test date:			
Examiner(s):			

B. Communicative Understanding *(continued)*	Target	Score	Notes	Score	Notes	Score	Notes
3. Follows multistep directions without contextual cues			C M Q R		C M Q R		C M Q R
3.1 Follows multistep directions with contextual cues			C M Q R		C M Q R		C M Q R
3.2 Follows one-step direction without contextual cues			C M Q R		C M Q R		C M Q R
3.3 Follows one-step direction with contextual cues			C M Q R		C M Q R		C M Q R
4. Responds to comprehension questions related to *why*, *how*, and *when*			C M Q R		C M Q R		C M Q R
4.1 Answers *who*, *what*, and *where* questions			C M Q R		C M Q R		C M Q R
C. Communicative Expression							
1. Produces multiple-word sentences to communicate			C M Q R		C M Q R		C M Q R
1.1 Uses two-word utterances			C M Q R		C M Q R		C M Q R
1.2 Uses 50 single words, signs, or symbols			C M Q R		C M Q R		C M Q R
1.3 Uses consistent approximations for words or signs			C M Q R		C M Q R		C M Q R
1.4 Uses consistent consonant-vowel combinations			C M Q R		C M Q R		C M Q R
2. Uses plural pronouns to indicate subjects, objects, and possession in multiple-word sentences			C M Q R		C M Q R		C M Q R
2.1 Uses irregular plural nouns in multiple-word sentences			C M Q R		C M Q R		C M Q R
2.2 Uses regular plural nouns			C M Q R		C M Q R		C M Q R
3. Uses helping verbs			C M Q R		C M Q R		C M Q R
3.1 Uses irregular past tense of common verbs			C M Q R		C M Q R		C M Q R
3.2 Uses regular past tense of common verbs			C M Q R		C M Q R		C M Q R
3.3 Uses *to be* verbs			C M Q R		C M Q R		C M Q R
4. Asks questions using inverted auxiliary			C M Q R		C M Q R		C M Q R
4.1 Asks *wh-* questions			C M Q R		C M Q R		C M Q R

Assessment, Evaluation, and Programming System for Infants and Children, Third Edition (AEPS®-3),
by Bricker, Dionne, Grisham, Johnson, Macy, Slentz, & Waddell. © 2022 Brookes Publishing Co. All rights reserved.

CHILD OBSERVATION DATA FORM

Social-Communication

aeps 3

Score Key			Note Key
Mastery performance 2	Emerging performance 1A = Assistance 1I = Incomplete 1AI = Assistance/Incomplete	No performance 0	C = Conduct M = Modification Q = Quality R = Report

Test date:			
Examiner(s):			

D. Social Use of Language	Target	Score	Notes	Score	Notes	Score	Notes
1. Uses language to initiate and sustain social interaction			C M Q R		C M Q R		C M Q R
1.1 Follows social conventions of language			C M Q R		C M Q R		C M Q R
2. Provides and seeks information while conversing using words, phrases, or sentences			C M Q R		C M Q R		C M Q R
2.1 Asks questions to obtain information			C M Q R		C M Q R		C M Q R
2.2 Describes objects, people, and events as part of social exchange			C M Q R		C M Q R		C M Q R
3. Uses conversational rules when communicating with others			C M Q R		C M Q R		C M Q R
3.1 Uses socially appropriate physical orientation			C M Q R		C M Q R		C M Q R
3.2 Varies voice to impart meaning and recognize social or environmental conditions			C M Q R		C M Q R		C M Q R
3.3 Responds to topic initiations from others			C M Q R		C M Q R		C M Q R
3.4 Alternates between speaker and listener roles during conversations with others			C M Q R		C M Q R		C M Q R
3.5 Responds to contingent questions from others			C M Q R		C M Q R		C M Q R

Social-Communication Results

To calculate Area Raw Score: Add the 2 and 1 scores in the Score column for the specific test date.
To calculate Area Percent Score: Divide the Area Raw Score by the Area Raw Score Possible, then multiply by 100.

Test date			
Area Raw Score			
Area Raw Score Possible	98	98	98
Area Percent Score			

Assessment, Evaluation, and Programming System for Infants and Children, Third Edition (AEPS®-3),
by Bricker, Dionne, Grisham, Johnson, Macy, Slentz, & Waddell. © 2022 Brookes Publishing Co. All rights reserved.

Social-Communication

Name: ______________________________

TEST DATE 1:

Examiner(s):

Comments:

TEST DATE 2:

Examiner(s):

Comments:

TEST DATE 3:

Examiner(s):

Comments:

Assessment, Evaluation, and Programming System for Infants and Children, Third Edition (AEPS®-3),
by Bricker, Dionne, Grisham, Johnson, Macy, Slentz, & Waddell. © 2022 Brookes Publishing Co. All rights reserved.

CHILD OBSERVATION DATA FORM

Cognitive

aeps®3

Name: ______________________________

Score Key			Note Key
Mastery performance 2	Emerging performance 1A = Assistance 1I = Incomplete 1AI = Assistance/Incomplete	No performance 0	C = Conduct M = Modification Q = Quality R = Report

Test date:			
Examiner(s):			

A. Sensory Exploration	Target	Score	Notes	Score	Notes	Score	Notes
1. Orients to events or stimulation			C M Q R		C M Q R		C M Q R
1.1 Reacts to events or stimulation			C M Q R		C M Q R		C M Q R
2. Combines simple actions to examine people, animals, and objects			C M Q R		C M Q R		C M Q R
2.1 Uses sensory means to explore people, animals, and objects			C M Q R		C M Q R		C M Q R
B. Imitation and Memory							
1. Imitates novel coordinated motor actions			C M Q R		C M Q R		C M Q R
1.1 Imitates novel simple motor action not already in repertoire			C M Q R		C M Q R		C M Q R
1.2 Imitates familiar simple motor action			C M Q R		C M Q R		C M Q R
2. Imitates novel words			C M Q R		C M Q R		C M Q R
2.1 Imitates novel vocalizations			C M Q R		C M Q R		C M Q R
2.2 Imitates familiar vocalizations			C M Q R		C M Q R		C M Q R
3. Relates past events			C M Q R		C M Q R		C M Q R
3.1 Relates recent events without contextual cues			C M Q R		C M Q R		C M Q R
3.2 Relates recent events with contextual cues			C M Q R		C M Q R		C M Q R
3.3 Relates events immediately after they occur			C M Q R		C M Q R		C M Q R
C. Conceptual Knowledge							
1. Maintains search for object not in its usual location			C M Q R		C M Q R		C M Q R
1.1 Locates object in second of two hiding places			C M Q R		C M Q R		C M Q R
1.2 Locates hidden object			C M Q R		C M Q R		C M Q R
2. Recognizes symbols			C M Q R		C M Q R		C M Q R
2.1 Uses object to represent another object			C M Q R		C M Q R		C M Q R

Assessment, Evaluation, and Programming System for Infants and Children, Third Edition (AEPS®-3),
by Bricker, Dionne, Grisham, Johnson, Macy, Slentz, & Waddell. © 2022 Brookes Publishing Co. All rights reserved.

Cognitive

Score Key			Note Key
Mastery performance 2	Emerging performance 1A = Assistance 1I = Incomplete 1AI = Assistance/Incomplete	No performance 0	C = Conduct M = Modification Q = Quality R = Report

Test date:			
Examiner(s):			

C. Conceptual Knowledge *(continued)*	Target	Score	Notes	Score	Notes	Score	Notes
3. Classifies using multiple attributes			C M Q R		C M Q R		C M Q R
3.1 Classifies according to function			C M Q R		C M Q R		C M Q R
3.2 Classifies according to physical attribute			C M Q R		C M Q R		C M Q R
3.3 Discriminates between objects or people using common attributes			C M Q R		C M Q R		C M Q R
4. Uses early conceptual comparisons			C M Q R		C M Q R		C M Q R
4.1 Identifies common concepts			C M Q R		C M Q R		C M Q R
4.2 Identifies concrete concepts			C M Q R		C M Q R		C M Q R
D. Reasoning							
1. Uses object to obtain another object			C M Q R		C M Q R		C M Q R
1.1 Uses part of object or support to obtain another object			C M Q R		C M Q R		C M Q R
1.2 Retains one object when second object is obtained			C M Q R		C M Q R		C M Q R
2. Coordinates actions with objects to achieve new outcomes			C M Q R		C M Q R		C M Q R
2.1 Tries different simple actions to achieve goal			C M Q R		C M Q R		C M Q R
2.2 Uses simple actions on objects			C M Q R		C M Q R		C M Q R
3. Solves problems using multiple strategies			C M Q R		C M Q R		C M Q R
3.1 Evaluates common solutions to solve problems or reach goals			C M Q R		C M Q R		C M Q R
4. Draws plausible conclusions about events beyond personal experience			C M Q R		C M Q R		C M Q R
4.1 Draws conclusions about causes of events based on personal experience			C M Q R		C M Q R		C M Q R

Assessment, Evaluation, and Programming System for Infants and Children, Third Edition (AEPS®-3),
by Bricker, Dionne, Grisham, Johnson, Macy, Slentz, & Waddell. © 2022 Brookes Publishing Co. All rights reserved.

Cognitive

aeps3

Score Key			Note Key
Mastery performance 2	Emerging performance 1A = Assistance 1I = Incomplete 1AI = Assistance/Incomplete	No performance 0	C = Conduct M = Modification Q = Quality R = Report

Test date:			
Examiner(s):			

E. Scientific Discovery	Target	Score	Notes	Score	Notes	Score	Notes
1. Expands simple observations and explorations into further inquiry			C M Q R		C M Q R		C M Q R
1.1 Uses simple tools to gather information			C M Q R		C M Q R		C M Q R
1.2 Uses senses to explore			C M Q R		C M Q R		C M Q R
2. Anticipates outcome of investigation			C M Q R		C M Q R		C M Q R
2.1 Generates specific questions for investigation			C M Q R		C M Q R		C M Q R
2.2 Demonstrates knowledge about natural happenings			C M Q R		C M Q R		C M Q R
2.3 Makes observations			C M Q R		C M Q R		C M Q R
3. Investigates to test hypotheses			C M Q R		C M Q R		C M Q R
3.1 Draws on prior knowledge to guide investigations			C M Q R		C M Q R		C M Q R
3.2 Manipulates materials to cause change			C M Q R		C M Q R		C M Q R
4. Transfers knowledge			C M Q R		C M Q R		C M Q R
4.1 Communicates results of investigations			C M Q R		C M Q R		C M Q R
4.2 Demonstrates knowledge of properties of change resulting from investigations			C M Q R		C M Q R		C M Q R
4.3 Shows awareness that manipulation of materials or processes prompted change in those materials or processes			C M Q R		C M Q R		C M Q R

Cognitive Results

To calculate Area Raw Score: Add the 2 and 1 scores in the Score column for the specific test date.
To calculate Area Percent Score: Divide the Area Raw Score by the Area Raw Score Possible, then multiply by 100.

Test date			
Area Raw Score			
Area Raw Score Possible	100	100	100
Area Percent Score			

Assessment, Evaluation, and Programming System for Infants and Children, Third Edition (AEPS®-3),
by Bricker, Dionne, Grisham, Johnson, Macy, Slentz, & Waddell. © 2022 Brookes Publishing Co. All rights reserved.

Cognitive

Name: ______________________________

TEST DATE 1:

Examiner(s):

Comments:

TEST DATE 2:

Examiner(s):

Comments:

TEST DATE 3:

Examiner(s):

Comments:

Assessment, Evaluation, and Programming System for Infants and Children, Third Edition (AEPS®-3),
by Bricker, Dionne, Grisham, Johnson, Macy, Slentz, & Waddell. © 2022 Brookes Publishing Co. All rights reserved.

Literacy

Name: ______________________

Score Key			Note Key
Mastery performance 2	Emerging performance 1A = Assistance 1I = Incomplete 1AI = Assistance/Incomplete	No performance 0	C = Conduct M = Modification Q = Quality R = Report

Test date:			
Examiner(s):			

A. Awareness of Print Concepts	Target	Score	Notes	Score	Notes	Score	Notes
1. Participates in shared group reading			C M Q R		C M Q R		C M Q R
1.1 Participates in shared one-on-one reading			C M Q R		C M Q R		C M Q R
2. Demonstrates understanding that text is read in one direction and from top to bottom of page			C M Q R		C M Q R		C M Q R
2.1 Turns pages of book from beginning toward end			C M Q R		C M Q R		C M Q R
2.2 Holds book or other printed material with pictures correctly oriented			C M Q R		C M Q R		C M Q R
3. Recognizes print words for common or familiar people, objects, or pictures			C M Q R		C M Q R		C M Q R
3.1 Recognizes own first name in print			C M Q R		C M Q R		C M Q R
3.2 Recognizes common signs and logos			C M Q R		C M Q R		C M Q R
B. Phonological Awareness							
1. Produces rhyming words given oral prompt			C M Q R		C M Q R		C M Q R
1.1 Identifies rhyming words			C M Q R		C M Q R		C M Q R
1.2 Participates in repetitive verbal play			C M Q R		C M Q R		C M Q R
2. Segments compound words into component words			C M Q R		C M Q R		C M Q R
2.1 Blends two simple words into compound words			C M Q R		C M Q R		C M Q R
2.2 Claps for words in sentences			C M Q R		C M Q R		C M Q R
3. Segments syllables of two- and three-syllable words			C M Q R		C M Q R		C M Q R
3.1 Blends syllables into two- and three-syllable words			C M Q R		C M Q R		C M Q R
3.2 Claps for each syllable in two- and three-syllable words			C M Q R		C M Q R		C M Q R
4. Segments CVC words into individual sounds			C M Q R		C M Q R		C M Q R
4.1 Blends separate CVC sounds into simple words			C M Q R		C M Q R		C M Q R
4.2 Identifies middle sounds in CVC words			C M Q R		C M Q R		C M Q R

Assessment, Evaluation, and Programming System for Infants and Children, Third Edition (AEPS®-3),
by Bricker, Dionne, Grisham, Johnson, Macy, Slentz, & Waddell. © 2022 Brookes Publishing Co. All rights reserved.

Literacy

aeps-3

Score Key			Note Key
Mastery performance 2	Emerging performance 1A = Assistance 1I = Incomplete 1AI = Assistance/Incomplete	No performance 0	C = Conduct M = Modification Q = Quality R = Report

Test date:			
Examiner(s):			

B. Phonological Awareness *(continued)*	Target	Score	Notes	Score	Notes	Score	Notes
4.3 Identifies last sounds in CVC words			C M Q R		C M Q R		C M Q R
4.4 Identifies beginning sounds in CVC words			C M Q R		C M Q R		C M Q R
4.5 Produces words that begin with specified sound			C M Q R		C M Q R		C M Q R
C. Alphabet Knowledge							
1. Names all uppercase and lowercase letters of alphabet			C M Q R		C M Q R		C M Q R
1.1 Matches frequently occurring lowercase letters with uppercase counterparts			C M Q R		C M Q R		C M Q R
1.2 Names 12 frequently occurring letters			C M Q R		C M Q R		C M Q R
1.3 Recognizes five frequently occurring letters not in first name			C M Q R		C M Q R		C M Q R
1.4 Names letters in own first name			C M Q R		C M Q R		C M Q R
1.5 Recognizes three letters in own first name			C M Q R		C M Q R		C M Q R
2. Reads simple CVC and sight word text			C M Q R		C M Q R		C M Q R
2.1 Sounds out CVC words			C M Q R		C M Q R		C M Q R
2.2 Reads frequently occurring sight words			C M Q R		C M Q R		C M Q R
2.3 Produces correct sounds for 20 letters of alphabet			C M Q R		C M Q R		C M Q R
2.4 Produces correct sounds for six letters of alphabet			C M Q R		C M Q R		C M Q R
D. Vocabulary and Story Comprehension							
1. Demonstrates understanding that pictures represent text			C M Q R		C M Q R		C M Q R
1.1 Labels familiar people, actions, objects, and events in picture books			C M Q R		C M Q R		C M Q R
1.2 Locates familiar objects, people, events, and actions in picture books			C M Q R		C M Q R		C M Q R
1.3 Matches pictures to actual objects, people, or actions			C M Q R		C M Q R		C M Q R

Assessment, Evaluation, and Programming System for Infants and Children, Third Edition (AEPS®-3),
by Bricker, Dionne, Grisham, Johnson, Macy, Slentz, & Waddell. © 2022 Brookes Publishing Co. All rights reserved.

Literacy

Score Key			Note Key
Mastery performance 2	Emerging performance 1A = Assistance 1I = Incomplete 1AI = Assistance/Incomplete	No performance 0	C = Conduct M = Modification Q = Quality R = Report

Test date:			
Examiner(s):			

D. Vocabulary and Story Comprehension *(continued)*	Target	Score	Notes	Score	Notes	Score	Notes
2. Retells simple story			C M Q R		C M Q R		C M Q R
2.1 Makes predictions about what will happen next in story			C M Q R		C M Q R		C M Q R
2.2 Answers and asks questions related to story			C M Q R		C M Q R		C M Q R
2.3 Tells story associated with series of pictures			C M Q R		C M Q R		C M Q R
3. Demonstrates understanding of abstract story vocabulary			C M Q R		C M Q R		C M Q R
3.1 Demonstrates understanding of key vocabulary in picture books			C M Q R		C M Q R		C M Q R
3.2 Demonstrates understanding of title, author, and illustrator			C M Q R		C M Q R		C M Q R
3.3 Demonstrates understanding of vocabulary associated with early literacy concepts			C M Q R		C M Q R		C M Q R
E. Writing							
1. "Reads" back own dictation to label or caption picture			C M Q R		C M Q R		C M Q R
1.1 Dictates description of drawing			C M Q R		C M Q R		C M Q R
1.2 Verbally labels representational drawings			C M Q R		C M Q R		C M Q R
1.3 Verbally labels nonrepresentational drawings			C M Q R		C M Q R		C M Q R
2. Writes and draws for a variety of purposes			C M Q R		C M Q R		C M Q R
2.1 Makes representational drawings			C M Q R		C M Q R		C M Q R
3. Writes words using conventional spelling			C M Q R		C M Q R		C M Q R
3.1 Writes using developmental spelling			C M Q R		C M Q R		C M Q R
3.2 Prints first name			C M Q R		C M Q R		C M Q R
3.3 Copies entire first name			C M Q R		C M Q R		C M Q R
3.4 Writes using "scribble writing"			C M Q R		C M Q R		C M Q R

Assessment, Evaluation, and Programming System for Infants and Children, Third Edition (AEPS®-3),
by Bricker, Dionne, Grisham, Johnson, Macy, Slentz, & Waddell. © 2022 Brookes Publishing Co. All rights reserved

Literacy Results

To calculate Area Raw Score: Add the 2 and 1 scores in the Score column for the specific test date.
To calculate Area Percent Score: Divide the Area Raw Score by the Area Raw Score Possible, then multiply by 100.

Test date			
Area Raw Score			
Area Raw Score Possible	114	114	114
Area Percent Score			

Assessment, Evaluation, and Programming System for Infants and Children, Third Edition (AEPS®-3),
by Bricker, Dionne, Grisham, Johnson, Macy, Slentz, & Waddell. © 2022 Brookes Publishing Co. All rights reserved.

Literacy

Name: ______________________________

TEST DATE 1:

Examiner(s):

Comments:

TEST DATE 2:

Examiner(s):

Comments:

TEST DATE 3:

Examiner(s):

Comments:

Assessment, Evaluation, and Programming System for Infants and Children, Third Edition (AEPS®-3),
by Bricker, Dionne, Grisham, Johnson, Macy, Slentz, & Waddell. © 2022 Brookes Publishing Co. All rights reserved.

CHILD OBSERVATION DATA FORM

Math

aeps-3

Name: ______________________________

Score Key			Note Key
Mastery performance 2	Emerging performance 1A = Assistance 1I = Incomplete 1AI = Assistance/Incomplete	No performance 0	C = Conduct M = Modification Q = Quality R = Report

Test date:			
Examiner(s):			

A. Counting	Target	Score	Notes	Score	Notes	Score	Notes
1. Counts out 3 items			C M Q R		C M Q R		C M Q R
1.1 Counts 3 items to determine "How many?"			C M Q R		C M Q R		C M Q R
1.2 Recites numbers 1-3			C M Q R		C M Q R		C M Q R
2. Counts out 10 items			C M Q R		C M Q R		C M Q R
2.1 Counts 10 items to determine "How many?"			C M Q R		C M Q R		C M Q R
2.2 Recites numbers 1-10			C M Q R		C M Q R		C M Q R
3. Counts out 20 items			C M Q R		C M Q R		C M Q R
3.1 Counts 20 items to determine "How many?"			C M Q R		C M Q R		C M Q R
3.2 Recites numbers 1-20			C M Q R		C M Q R		C M Q R
4. Skip counts by tens to 100			C M Q R		C M Q R		C M Q R
4.1 Recites numbers 31-100			C M Q R		C M Q R		C M Q R
4.2 Recites numbers 1-30			C M Q R		C M Q R		C M Q R
B. Quantitative Relations							
1. Compares items in sets to 5 by counting			C M Q R		C M Q R		C M Q R
1.1 Compares items in sets to 5 by matching			C M Q R		C M Q R		C M Q R
1.2 Creates equivalent sets of 5 items			C M Q R		C M Q R		C M Q R
1.3 Uses quantity comparison words			C M Q R		C M Q R		C M Q R
2. Compares items in sets of 6 to 10 by counting			C M Q R		C M Q R		C M Q R
2.1 Compares items in sets of 6 to 10 by matching			C M Q R		C M Q R		C M Q R
2.2 Creates equivalent sets of 10 items			C M Q R		C M Q R		C M Q R

Assessment, Evaluation, and Programming System for Infants and Children, Third Edition (AEPS®-3),
by Bricker, Dionne, Grisham, Johnson, Macy, Slentz, & Waddell. © 2022 Brookes Publishing Co. All rights reserved.

aeps3

Score Key			Note Key
Mastery performance 2	Emerging performance 1A = Assistance 1I = Incomplete 1AI = Assistance/Incomplete	No performance 0	C = Conduct M = Modification Q = Quality R = Report

Test date:			
Examiner(s):			

B. Quantitative Relations *(continued)*	Target	Score	Notes	Score	Notes	Score	Notes
3. Compares items in sets of 11 to 20 by counting			C M Q R		C M Q R		C M Q R
3.1 Compares items in sets of 11 to 20 by matching			C M Q R		C M Q R		C M Q R
3.2 Compares items in sets of 11 to 20 by visual examination			C M Q R		C M Q R		C M Q R
C. Reading and Writing Numbers							
1. Reads and writes numerals for quantities to 5			C M Q R		C M Q R		C M Q R
1.1 Demonstrates understanding of mathematical meaning of written numerals *1–5*			C M Q R		C M Q R		C M Q R
1.2 Labels numerals *1–5*			C M Q R		C M Q R		C M Q R
2. Reads and writes numerals for quantities 6–10			C M Q R		C M Q R		C M Q R
2.1 Demonstrates understanding of mathematical meaning of written numerals *6–10*			C M Q R		C M Q R		C M Q R
2.2 Labels numerals *6–10*			C M Q R		C M Q R		C M Q R
3. Reads and writes numerals for quantities 11–20			C M Q R		C M Q R		C M Q R
3.1 Demonstrates understanding of mathematical meaning of written numerals *11–20*			C M Q R		C M Q R		C M Q R
3.2 Labels numerals *11–20*			C M Q R		C M Q R		C M Q R
D. Addition and Subtraction							
1. Reads and writes symbols for addition (+) and equals (=)			C M Q R		C M Q R		C M Q R
1.1 Solves picture or object addition problems using shortcut sum strategy			C M Q R		C M Q R		C M Q R
1.2 Counts forward to 10			C M Q R		C M Q R		C M Q R
1.3 Solves picture or object problems using count all strategy			C M Q R		C M Q R		C M Q R
1.4 Says number after 1–10			C M Q R		C M Q R		C M Q R
1.5 Demonstrates understanding of concept of addition			C M Q R		C M Q R		C M Q R

Assessment, Evaluation, and Programming System for Infants and Children, Third Edition (AEPS®-3),
by Bricker, Dionne, Grisham, Johnson, Macy, Slentz, & Waddell. © 2022 Brookes Publishing Co. All rights reserved.

Math

Score Key			Note Key
Mastery performance 2	Emerging performance 1A = Assistance 1I = Incomplete 1AI = Assistance/Incomplete	No performance 0	C = Conduct M = Modification Q = Quality R = Report

Test date:			
Examiner(s):			

D. Addition and Subtraction *(continued)*	Target	Score	Notes	Score	Notes	Score	Notes
2. Reads and writes symbols for subtraction (–) and equals (=)			C M Q R		C M Q R		C M Q R
2.1 Solves picture or object subtraction problems with set of 10 or less			C M Q R		C M Q R		C M Q R
2.2 Says number before 2–10			C M Q R		C M Q R		C M Q R
2.3 Demonstrates understanding of concept of subtraction			C M Q R		C M Q R		C M Q R

Math Results

To calculate Area Raw Score: Add the 2 and 1 scores in the Score column for the specific test date.

To calculate Area Percent Score: Divide the Area Raw Score by the Area Raw Score Possible, then multiply by 100.

Test date			
Area Raw Score			
Area Raw Score Possible	82	82	82
Area Percent Score			

Assessment, Evaluation, and Programming System for Infants and Children, Third Edition (AEPS®-3),
by Bricker, Dionne, Grisham, Johnson, Macy, Slentz, & Waddell. © 2022 Brookes Publishing Co. All rights reserved.

Math

aeps-3

Name: ____

TEST DATE 1:

Examiner(s):

Comments:

TEST DATE 2:

Examiner(s):

Comments:

TEST DATE 3:

Examiner(s):

Comments:

Assessment, Evaluation, and Programming System for Infants and Children, Third Edition (AEPS®-3),
by Bricker, Dionne, Grisham, Johnson, Macy, Slentz, & Waddell. © 2022 Brookes Publishing Co. All rights reserved.

Summary of AEPS-3 Results

aeps3

Name: ______________________________

For each area, plot the percent correct and indicate each test date to determine if the child's performance is improving over time.

Fine Motor			
Total % correct 100			
80			
60			
40			
20			
Test date:			

Gross Motor			
Total % correct 100			
80			
60			
40			
20			
Test date:			

Adaptive			
Total % correct 100			
80			
60			
40			
20			
Test date:			

Social-Emotional			
Total % correct 100			
80			
60			
40			
20			
Test date:			

Social-Communication			
Total % correct 100			
80			
60			
40			
20			
Test date:			

Cognitive			
Total % correct 100			
80			
60			
40			

Literacy			
Total % correct 100			
80			
60			
40			
20			
Test date:			

DO NOT BREAK.
These forms are not sold individually. They are available only as a set. Resellers should not open shrink-wrapped sets.

ISBN-13: 978-1-68125-527-9
ISBN-10: 1-68125-527-8
90000
9 781681 255279